EVOLUTION

The incredible story of life on E

by Matthew Rake

Illustrated by Peter Minister

HUNGRY
BANANA

CONTENTS

mya means 'million years ago'

How do we know this stuff?

Scientists who study the history of living things are known as palaeontologists. To learn about life in the past, they find and study fossils. These are simply the remains of animals and plants that have been preserved in rocks.

There are two types of fossil: body fossils and trace fossils. A body fossil preserves the actual parts of an animal or plant. A trace fossil preserves the marks that organisms have made. For example, an animal may have made a burrow or footprints, or a plant may have left holes where its roots once were.

Hi, My name is Ackerley and I'm an Acanthostega.

I'm your guide in this book and I've got the world's greatest story to tell you – how life evolved on Earth. Or, to put it another way...

...how we all got here.

We're going to find out how tiny, microscopic organisms evolved into huge dinosaurs. And I'll even tell you how you lot, *homo sapiens*, came into being.

But, you guys have only been around for about 200,000 years, and the world is 4,500 million years old. So this is a big story. We start by seeing how the Earth was formed from gas, dust and rocks, and how it became a watery place. You'll meet the first animals (all from the sea) and some of the scariest creatures of the deep!

Opabinia, page 14

The first land animal was a tiny millipede. Creatures like this thrived as Earth's atmosphere became filled with oxygen, and plants provided a food source. Meanwhile, fish started to develop lungs and legs so that they could live on land.

This is where I come in.

You see, we Acanthostegas were one of the first species to make a (scrambling!) move from water on to land. (And we still stayed close to the water!)

Spinosaurus, page 50

Liopleurodon, page 44

We'll travel on in time and reach the Triassic and Jurassic periods, when Earth's reptiles evolved into an amazing variety of creatures. Some developed wings and became aerial assassins; others moved into the oceans and became ferocious sea monsters. Many reptiles evolved into savage dinosaurs, some as big as double-decker buses...

...or bigger!

The Cretaceous period was ruled by huge, scary beasts, such as T. rex and Spinosaurus, but there were gentler creatures, too, like Maiasaura.

We'll find out how the Cretaceous ended with a mighty bang, causing many animals to die out completely. When the mammals evolved, some were every bit as frightening as the dinosaurs. But...

...it's not just mammals that were scary.

Terror birds, taller than humans and with huge, pointed beaks, became the top predators in South America...

So hold tight and keep reading!

Paraceratherium, page 77

The changing shape of the planet

You may think the map of the world has always looked the same. But the continents have changed dramatically throughout the history of the Earth, just as animals and plants have. About 225 million years ago, the whole world was one big supercontinent called Pangaea.

About 225 million years ago

Pangaea

About 200 million years ago, the continent of Pangaea was dividing into Laurasia in the north and Gondwanaland in the south.

About 200 million years ago

Laurasia

Gondwanaland

By about 66 million years ago, when the dinosaurs were wiped out, the world was looking much more like it does today. Laurasia was splitting up into North America in the west and Europe and Asia in the east. Gondwanaland had split into South America, Africa, India and Antarctica/Australia.

About 66 million years ago

In the last 66 million years, North and South America have joined up, Antarctica and Australia separated, and India merged with the continent of Asia.

EVOLUTION TIMELINE

Precambrian

The story begins with the Big Bang 15,000 million years ago (mya). Life on Earth starts around 3,800 mya. Oxygen forms in the atmosphere about 2,300 mya as a waste product of photosynthesizing bacteria, in what scientists call the Great Oxygenation Event. The ozone layer begins forming above the Earth 600 mya - this will eventually protect the Earth from the harmful rays of the sun. These events mean that animals will ultimately be able to live on land.

Cambrian

Sea animals start appearing in the 'Cambrian explosion of life' 540-520 mya. They swim, crawl, burrow, hunt, defend themselves and hide away. Some creatures evolve hard parts such as shells.

Devonian

Life begins on land, as plants grow by lakes, streams and coasts, and arthropods (animals with segmented bodies, like millipedes) venture onto land. The first jawed fish appear.

Carboniferous

The first reptiles evolve from one branch of amphibians. Reptiles are the first animals with backbones to live permanently on land. Vast forests cover the Earth, and these will eventually fossilize and become coal.

Precambrian 4,540-541 mya	Cambrian 541-485 mya	Ordovician 485-443 mya	Silurian 443-419 mya	Devonian 419-359 mya	Carboniferous 359-299 mya

The 'golden age of the dinosaurs' witnesses huge herbivore dinosaurs feeding on lush ferns and palm-like cycads. Smaller but vicious meat-eating dinosaurs hunt the great herbivores.

Homo sapiens appears in Africa around 200,000 years ago. By 35,000 years ago, humans also live in Europe, southern Asia and Australia. Around 15,000 years ago, they move into North America.

Dinosaurs appear, as do the first mammals and the first flying animals with backbones, the pterosaurs.

Many different mammals evolve – some stay on land; some, like whales, go back into the water; some, like monkeys, take to the trees.

Jurassic

Triassic

Cretaceous

Paleogene

Neogene

Quaternary

Permian 299-252 mya	Triassic 252-201 mya	Jurassic 201-145 mya	Cretaceous 145-66 mya	Paleogene 66-23 mya	Neogene 23-2.6 mya	Quaternary 2.6 mya - now

BIRTH OF THE EARTH

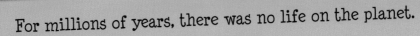

For millions of years, there was no life on the planet.

In fact, to begin with, there was no planet at all!

The Earth started off simply as dust and gas, spinning in a spiral. Gradually, it gathered more rocks from space, like a whirlpool funnelling more and more material into its centre.

With gravity pulling everything together, the Earth eventually became a solid planet: a great ball of molten rock and metal with a solid outer crust.

When the Earth first formed 4,540 million years ago, it was not exactly a great place for life. There was no water, no breathable air and no protection from the rays of the sun. From inside the planet, red-hot liquid rock, known as lava, spewed out in huge volcanic eruptions. On the outside, fiery meteorites bombarded the surface.

For life to begin, the Earth needed water. Today, water covers 70% of the Earth's surface. But where did it all come from?

Scientists once believed that, as the Earth was so hot, water must have come from outside the planet. Perhaps a comet, packed with ice, crashed into it. However, we can now analyse water evaporating off today's comets, and it is a different type from the Earth's.

So now many scientists think that water was trapped deep inside the planet, and was forced out as steam in the volcanic eruptions. Eventually, when the Earth cooled, the steam turned to liquid water.

Precambrian 4,540-541 mya

Cambrian 541-485 mya

Ordovician 485-443 mya

Silurian 443-419 mya

Devonian 419-359 mya

Carboniferous 359-299 mya

Permian 299-252 mya

Triassic 252-201 mya

Jurassic 201-145 mya

Cretaceous 145-66 mya

Paleogene 66-23 mya

Neogene 23-2.6 mya

Quaternary 2.6 mya - present

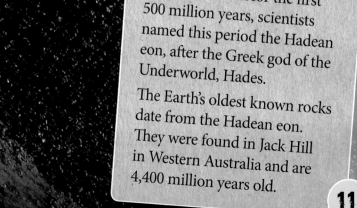

Did You Know?

As the world was full of fire and molten rock for the first 500 million years, scientists named this period the Hadean eon, after the Greek god of the Underworld, Hades.

The Earth's oldest known rocks date from the Hadean eon. They were found in Jack Hill in Western Australia and are 4,400 million years old.

HELL AND HIGH WATER

So how did this horribly hot and violent world change into the planet that we know, with forests, rivers and oceans bursting with all kinds of life? Well, the volcanoes created great clouds of steam; the steam collected in a thick blanket around the whole world;

and then it rained.

And when I say rain, I mean **rain** – a deluge that went on for thousands, perhaps even millions, of years! Think about that the next time you complain about getting caught in a passing shower.

All living things are made up of cells, the basic building blocks of life, and the first living things were composed of just one cell each. They are known as micro-organisms.

Scientists can't agree exactly where the first micro-organisms formed. Some think it was in shallow pools of seawater; some say in water droplets in the air. But the most recent theory is that life started at the bottom of the ocean, where boiling water shot up through vents from the centre of the Earth.

It doesn't sound a great place for life to exist, hundreds of metres down where no sunlight ever reaches. But the hot water bursting upwards would have carried minerals and energy to help. And anyway, the surface of the Earth was being bombarded by meteorites and covered with volcanic lava.

Today, we know that whole communities of living things – including micro-organisms, worms and giant clams – collect around the hot water of deep-sea vents.

Did You Know?

Many of the first micro-organisms, such as algae, became trapped in multiple layers of rock, known as stromatolites. In Australia, scientists have found stromatolites containing algae fossils from 3,500 million years ago. So you can actually see evidence of some of the first living things ever to appear on Earth.

13

A SEA CHANGE

If there were a prize for The Weirdest Creature That Ever Lived, **Opabinia** would be a hot favourite for the top spot. It had five mushroom-shaped eyes, 15 segments on its body, and a grasping claw at the end of a long nose (or proboscis to give it its scientific name). Opabinia used its extra proboscis to feed itself, much like an elephant uses its trunk. Perhaps it could even pull worms out of holes with its claw.

Opabinia

Another contestant for the prize of The Weirdest Creature That Ever Lived would definitely be **Hallucigenia** (right). When it was first studied in the 1970s, scientists thought it walked along the bottom of the seafloor on spiny stilts, and that waving tentacles grew on its back. But now experts think the tentacles were actually legs and the spines on its back provided protection. Turning it upside down might make more sense, but it still looks pretty strange!

It took about 3,000 million years for life to evolve from simple cells into soft-bodied sea animals.

That's about two-thirds of the whole age of the planet!

And what a strange-looking bunch of animals they were, when they finally did appear...

OPABINIA
Location: Canada
Length: 6cm (2.5in)

Precambrian
4,540-541 mya

Cambrian
541-485 mya

Ordovician
485-443 mya

Silurian
443-419 mya

Devonian
419-359 mya

Carboniferous
359-299 mya

Permian
299-252 mya

Triassic
252-201 mya

Jurassic
201-145 mya

Cretaceous
145-66 mya

Paleogene
66-23 mya

Neogene
23-2.6 mya

Quaternary
2.6 mya - present

Hallucigenia

Did You Know?
Many of the best fossils of the earliest animals come from Burgess Shale in the Rocky Mountains in Canada. In some, you can even see the food the animal last ate inside its body – and it's over 500 million years old!

15

SLAYERS IN THE SEA

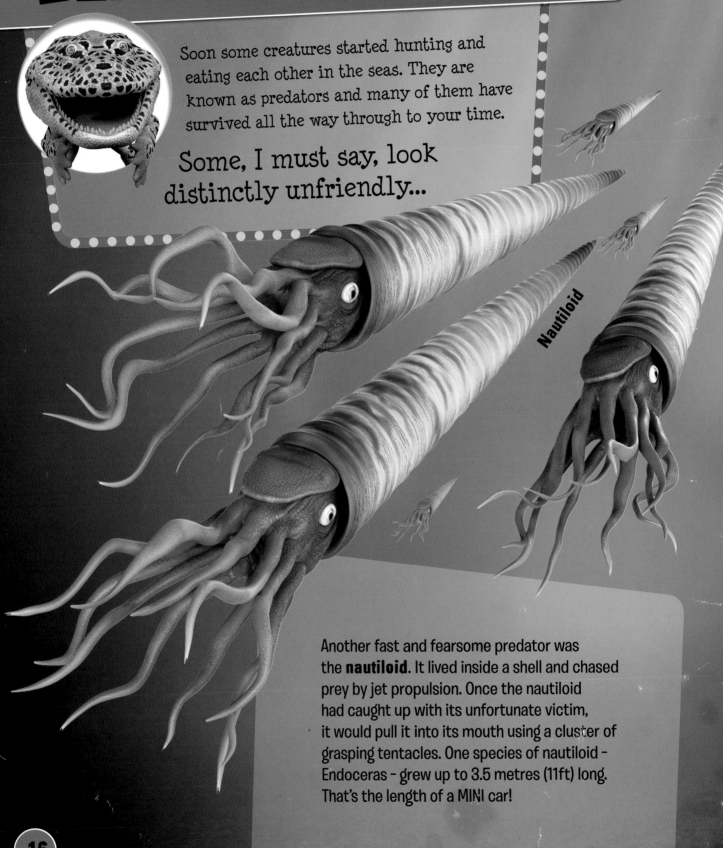

Soon some creatures started hunting and eating each other in the seas. They are known as predators and many of them have survived all the way through to your time.

Some, I must say, look distinctly unfriendly...

Nautiloid

Another fast and fearsome predator was the **nautiloid**. It lived inside a shell and chased prey by jet propulsion. Once the nautiloid had caught up with its unfortunate victim, it would pull it into its mouth using a cluster of grasping tentacles. One species of nautiloid - Endoceras - grew up to 3.5 metres (11ft) long. That's the length of a MINI car!

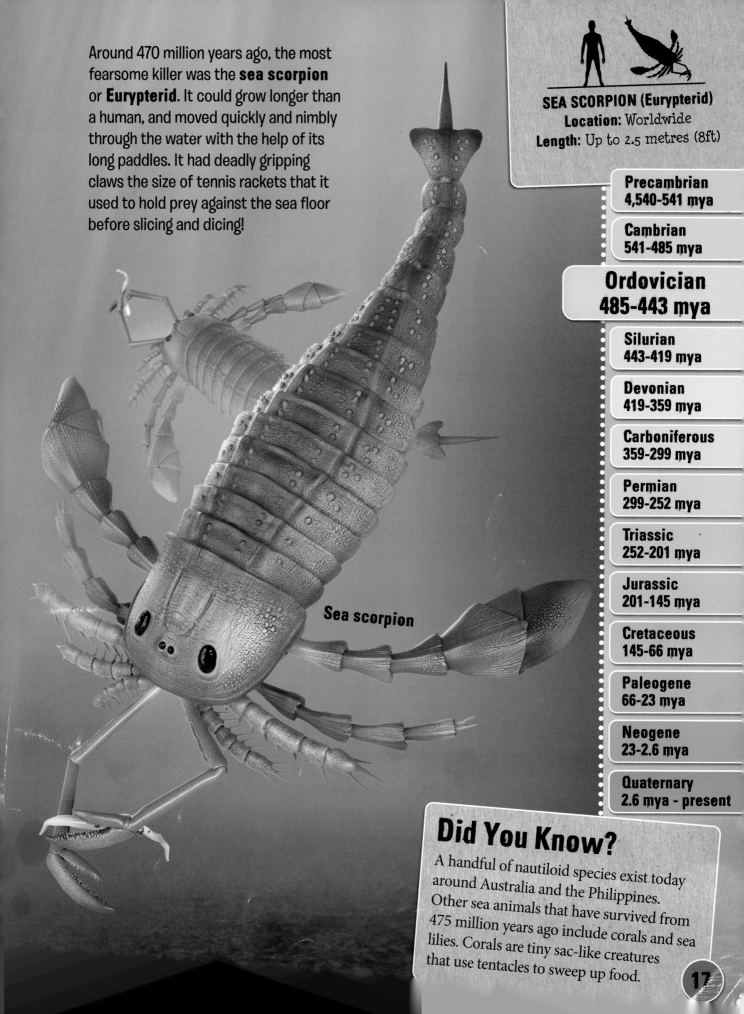

Around 470 million years ago, the most fearsome killer was the **sea scorpion** or **Eurypterid**. It could grow longer than a human, and moved quickly and nimbly through the water with the help of its long paddles. It had deadly gripping claws the size of tennis rackets that it used to hold prey against the sea floor before slicing and dicing!

SEA SCORPION (Eurypterid)
Location: Worldwide
Length: Up to 2.5 metres (8ft)

Precambrian
4,540-541 mya

Cambrian
541-485 mya

Ordovician
485-443 mya

Silurian
443-419 mya

Devonian
419-359 mya

Carboniferous
359-299 mya

Permian
299-252 mya

Triassic
252-201 mya

Jurassic
201-145 mya

Cretaceous
145-66 mya

Paleogene
66-23 mya

Neogene
23-2.6 mya

Quaternary
2.6 mya - present

Sea scorpion

Did You Know?

A handful of nautiloid species exist today around Australia and the Philippines. Other sea animals that have survived from 475 million years ago include corals and sea lilies. Corals are tiny sac-like creatures that use tentacles to sweep up food.

MONSTER OF THE DEEP

The first fish emerged around 510 million years ago. They were jawless and looked like giant tadpoles. Wriggling slowly along the seabed with their mouths open, they sucked up tiny animals. Over millions of years, though, they evolved jaws to bite with, forked tail fins for turning quickly, and bony heads for protection against predators, such as the sea scorpion (see previous page).

One of these bony-headed fish was the 4-tonne (8,818-lb) monster, **Dunkleosteus**. It had an armour-plated skull about 1.3 metres (4ft) wide. The plating itself was as much as 5cm (2in) thick, and the sharp edges of this plating served as teeth.

What's more, Dunkleosteus had some bite - its force has been estimated at 5,000 newtons (1,100lb). That's more powerful than the bite of a lion, tiger or hyena. Dunkleosteus could also open its mouth very quickly, in just one-fiftieth of a second, which created a strong suction force that pulled even fast-moving prey into its mouth.

DUNKLEOSTEUS
Location: Worldwide
Length: 6 metres (2oft)

Precambrian
4,540-541 mya

Cambrian
541-485 mya

Ordovician
485-443 mya

Silurian
443-419 mya

Devonian
419-359 mya

Carboniferous
359-299 mya

Permian
299-252 mya

Triassic
252-201 mya

Jurassic
201-145 mya

Cretaceous
145-66 mya

Paleogene
66-23 mya

Neogene
23-2.6 mya

Quaternary
2.6 mya - present

Dunkleosteus

WOW, look at this fellow - pretty scary, huh?

I'm a bit worried... this monstrosity lived at the same time as me and I'd fit straight into that mouth. No wonder my ancestors adapted to escape onto land!

Dunkleosteus did not have teeth. Instead, it chomped its food with the jagged edges of the bony plates around its head. These plates continued to grow as they were worn down by use. And as the top and bottom plates rubbed against each other, they were always kept sharp.

Did You Know?

Dunkleosteus skeletons often have scars that were made by the jaws of other Dunkleosteus, showing that this killer did not fear attacking its own kind!

19

FISH WITH FINGERS

Acanthostega

Recognize this good-looking guy?

Yes, it's me, hanging with some of my friends down by the riverbank. We were one of the first species to develop legs. This allowed us to get around in shallow pools and mud at the water's edge.

Scientists don't think that **Acanthostega**'s legs could have supported its body weight, so they believe it developed them (and its fingers) to move around shallow waters filled with plants and woody debris.

So why did some fish decide that life would be better on land than in water? During the Devonian period, the Earth became warmer and drier. This meant lakes and rivers became shallower, with less oxygen and food for the animals that lived under the surface.

Some fish, known as the 'fleshy fins' or 'lobe fins', had lungs as well as gills, so they could breathe oxygen from the air. They developed muscular fins to pull themselves through shallow waters and to new pools. After many generations, these fins turned into limbs.

Acanthostega evolved limbs and digits, but not ankles and knees strong enough to support the weight of its body, which means that walking on land would probably have been extremely difficult!

Slightly more successful was Ichthyostega, which lived at the same time as Acanthostega. It hauled itself from the water using its front limbs as crutches, like a seal moves on the land today.

ACANTHOSTEGA
Length: 60cm (2ft)
Weight: About 3kg (7lb)

Precambrian	4,540-541 mya
Cambrian	541-485 mya
Ordovician	485-443 mya
Silurian	443-419 mya
Devonian	**419-359 mya**
Carboniferous	359-299 mya
Permian	299-252 mya
Triassic	252-201 mya
Jurassic	201-145 mya
Cretaceous	145-66 mya
Paleogene	66-23 mya
Neogene	23-2.6 mya
Quaternary	2.6 mya - present

Did You Know?

Acanthostega and Ichthyostega were the first known tetrapods (animals with four feet). They were the ancestors of the earliest four-limbed animals with backbones.

21

For over 3,000 million years, all life on Earth existed in water. Creatures could not survive on land because of the harmful ultraviolet rays of the sun. However, algae in the water produced oxygen and this eventually created a protective ozone layer around the Earth.

Then plants and arthropods (animals with jointed legs) became adapted to living on land.

Now, this story has got legs...

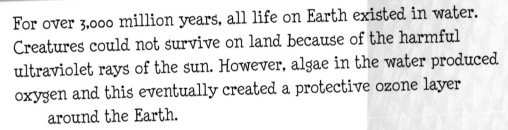

Millipedes thrived in the Carboniferous period because there was plenty of oxygen in the atmosphere and not many large predators. Some millipedes grew very, very large. **Arthropleura** became half the size of a modern-day crocodile!

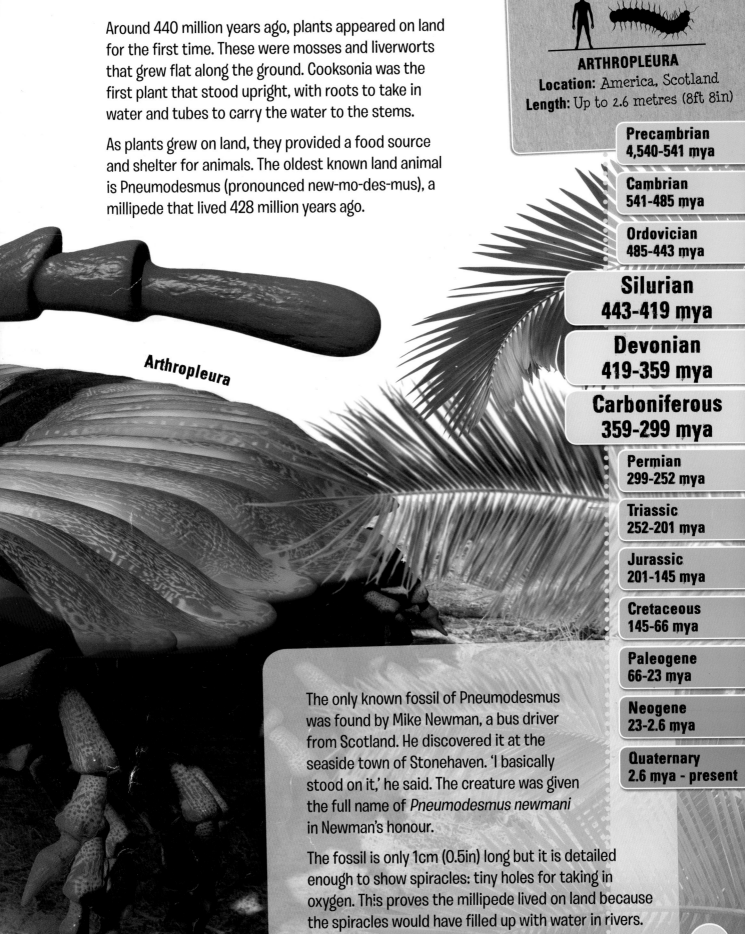

Around 440 million years ago, plants appeared on land for the first time. These were mosses and liverworts that grew flat along the ground. Cooksonia was the first plant that stood upright, with roots to take in water and tubes to carry the water to the stems.

As plants grew on land, they provided a food source and shelter for animals. The oldest known land animal is Pneumodesmus (pronounced new-mo-des-mus), a millipede that lived 428 million years ago.

Arthropleura

ARTHROPLEURA
Location: America, Scotland
Length: Up to 2.6 metres (8ft 8in)

Precambrian
4,540-541 mya

Cambrian
541-485 mya

Ordovician
485-443 mya

Silurian
443-419 mya

Devonian
419-359 mya

Carboniferous
359-299 mya

Permian
299-252 mya

Triassic
252-201 mya

Jurassic
201-145 mya

Cretaceous
145-66 mya

Paleogene
66-23 mya

Neogene
23-2.6 mya

Quaternary
2.6 mya - present

The only known fossil of Pneumodesmus was found by Mike Newman, a bus driver from Scotland. He discovered it at the seaside town of Stonehaven. 'I basically stood on it,' he said. The creature was given the full name of *Pneumodesmus newmani* in Newman's honour.

The fossil is only 1cm (0.5in) long but it is detailed enough to show spiracles: tiny holes for taking in oxygen. This proves the millipede lived on land because the spiracles would have filled up with water in rivers.

RISE OF THE REPTILES

He might look as big and ferocious as many dinosaurs, but **Dimetrodon** was actually a reptile that evolved from early tetrapods living about 50 million years before the dinosaurs. In fact, he was more like you mammals than a dinosaur. Here he seems to have a taste for tetrapods like me.

Thank goodness he wasn't around in my era...

...but 70 million years later!

Reptiles were the first vertebrates (animals with backbones) able to live on land all the time. They developed scales to stop them losing water through their skin and strong legs to move around easily.

Dimetrodon

The first reptile was Hylonomus. It lived 312 million years ago and was only 20cm (8in) long, including the tail. Dimetrodon lived about 30 million years later and was about 15 times as long, making it a fearsome predator.

People have debated why Dimetrodon had a 'sail' on its back. They once thought it might have given it camouflage among reeds where it waited for prey, or that it acted like the sail of a boat, catching the wind while Dimetrodon was in the water!

Experts now think the sail might have controlled Dimetrodon's body temperature. Cold-blooded reptiles need to warm up in the morning, so maybe the sail helped to soak up sunshine. Or perhaps, like the peacock's tail, it was a way of attracting mates.

DIMETRODON
Location: America and Europe
Length: About 3 metres (11ft)

Precambrian
4,540-541 mya

Cambrian
541-485 mya

Ordovician
485-443 mya

Silurian
443-419 mya

Devonian
419-359 mya

Carboniferous
359-299 mya

Permian
299-252 mya

Triassic
252-201 mya

Jurassic
201-145 mya

Cretaceous
145-66 mya

Paleogene
66-23 mya

Neogene
23-2.6 mya

Quaternary
2.6 mya - present

Dimetrodon means 'two shapes of tooth' in Greek. At the front of Dimetrodon's mouth were stabbing canines for piercing skin. At the back, its shearing teeth could slice through bone and tough muscle. These teeth curved backwards to trap prey in its mouth. The edges of all the teeth had small serrations like those of a steak knife.

Did You Know?

Reptiles such as Dimetrodon laid their eggs on dry land, not in water as earlier tetrapods did. Inside each shell a waterproof covering, called an amnion, protected the baby and stopped it drying out.

PACK ATTACK

Moschops was a reptile that did not look quite right. Its big, barrel-shaped body now seems too large for its short legs, tiny feet and little tail. However, being close to the ground meant it could graze on low-lying vegetation. And its sturdy build had another advantage: helping it withstand attacks, perhaps from a pack of cynodonts.

Moschops

The **cynodonts** (meaning 'dog tooth') were really mixed-up creatures. Some species were carnivores, some herbivores. Some were the size of a modern domestic cat, some as large as a wolf.

Carnivorous cynodonts were fast and fierce. They had pointed canine teeth that could tear off chunks of flesh. Since mammals have similar teeth, scientists believe they represent one of the first steps towards the evolution of mammals. Cynodonts also had powerful legs that grew under their body like a mammal's, rather than out at the sides like most reptiles'.

MOSCHOPS
Location: South African forests
Length: About 5 metres (16ft)

Cynodont

Moschops looks as if it should be able to protect itself. It was bigger than a hippo and had a strong, hard head. In fact, I'm told Moschops used their heads to butt each other and show their dominance. Well, it looks as if this particular Moschops could do with

head-butting some of those cynodonts...

Precambrian	4,540-541 mya
Cambrian	541-485 mya
Ordovician	485-443 mya
Silurian	443-419 mya
Devonian	419-359 mya
Carboniferous	359-299 mya
Permian	**299-252 mya**
Triassic	252-201 mya
Jurassic	201-145 mya
Cretaceous	145-66 mya
Paleogene	66-23 mya
Neogene	23-2.6 mya
Quaternary	2.6 mya - present

Did You Know?

During the 'Great Dying', the Permo-Triassic mass extinction of 252 mya, about 95% of all marine species became extinct. It enabled reptiles to rule the planet.

MEET THE MAMMALS

There were all kinds of creatures around in the Triassic period. Take this chap, **Hyperodapedon**: he might not look it, but he's a reptile. And just to confuse matters further, he has a beak like a ceratopsian dinosaur. The other little critters might look more familiar to you.

They are your ancestors

– some of the first-ever mammals to walk the Earth.

Megazostrodon

Although the Triassic period is known as the time when dinosaurs rose to dominance, it also saw the first mammals appear. Characteristically, mammals suckle their young with milk, have hair or fur, and are warm-blooded.

Scientists think little shrew-like **Megazostrodon**, which appeared about 210 million years ago, may have been one of the first mammals. They believe it suckled its young after they hatched. Of course, scientists can't be sure, because fossils do not tell us much about how the young fed, or whether an animal had fur or was warm-blooded.

You might think that Hyperodapedon would fancy a Megazostrodon morsel for lunch, especially given its fearsome beak. In fact, Hyperodapedon used this to break open the seeds of now-extinct plants called seed ferns. Once the husk was split open, the animal chewed the seed's softer insides at the back of its mouth so it could digest them easily.

MEGAZOSTRODON
Location: South African woods
Length: 10-12cm (4-5in)

| Precambrian 4,540-541 mya |
| Cambrian 541-485 mya |
| Ordovician 485-443 mya |
| Silurian 443-419 mya |
| Devonian 419-359 mya |
| Carboniferous 359-299 mya |
| Permian 299-252 mya |
| **Triassic 252-201 mya** |
| Jurassic 201-145 mya |
| Cretaceous 145-66 mya |
| Paleogene 66-23 mya |
| Neogene 23-2.6 mya |
| Quaternary 2.6 mya - present |

Hyperodapedon

Not many animals fed on seed ferns, so Hyperodapedon did not have to compete with other herbivores for food supplies. But, when seed ferns disappeared at the end of the Triassic period, so did Hyperodapedon.

SAVAGES IN THE SEA

When **ichthyosaurs** were around, squid and fish needed to make themselves scarce. These ferocious sea monsters had huge eyes for spotting their prey and solid ear bones to hear the vibrations they made. So no matter how gloomy the waters, ichthyosaurs would always find their next meal.

What's more, helped by their streamlined bodies, they could chase their prey at speeds up to an estimated 40 km/h (25 mph). No wonder ichthyosaurs were the top sea predators in the late Triassic and early Jurassic periods.

If you think this ichthyosaur looks like a dolphin, you'd be right. And it's probably no coincidence. Ichthyosaurs evolved from land reptiles that returned to the water. Their legs developed into fins that made them better swimmers. Around 200 million years later, dolphins did the same thing, evolving from land mammals that returned to the water.

The other creature here is **Tanystropheus**. It certainly doesn't look like a dolphin – more like a sauropod! Check out that neck...

... it's 3 metres (10ft) long!

Tanystropheus

Tanystropheus doesn't look quite so suited to life in the water. Its neck and tail made up three-quarters of its total length. In fact, some scientists think it spent most of its time on land, perched on rocks along the shoreline, snatching fish from the shallows - a bit like fishing with your neck instead of a rod!

Ichthyosaur

| Precambrian 4,540-541 mya |
| Cambrian 541-485 mya |
| Ordovician 485-443 mya |
| Silurian 443-419 mya |
| Devonian 419-359 mya |
| Carboniferous 359-299 mya |
| Permian 299-252 mya |
| **Triassic 252-201 mya** |
| Jurassic 201-145 mya |
| Cretaceous 145-66 mya |
| Paleogene 66-23 mya |
| Neogene 23-2.6 mya |
| Quaternary 2.6 mya - present |

The first ichthyosaur skeleton was found in 1811 on the cliffs of Dorset, England, by 12-year-old Mary Anning. With her dog Tray, she had gone looking for fossils after a period of storms. In 1823, she discovered the first complete skeleton of a plesiosaur, the reptile that took over from ichthyosaurs as the top sea predator.

Did You Know?

Ichthyosaurs had huge eyes. The Temnodontosaurus species had the biggest of all, measuring up to 26cm (10.5in) in diameter. That's bigger than a human skull! For comparison, a blue whale's eye is 15cm (6in) in diameter.

31

TINY TERRORS

The first dinosaurs appeared 230 million years ago. But they weren't huge monsters –

more like chicken-sized T.rexes.

Eoraptor here is about one metre (39in) long, including the tail – about half my size. Mind you, I wouldn't have gone anywhere near it. Just look at those vicious claws on three of its five fingers, and it had needle-sharp teeth.

The first dinosaurs were known as theropods, meaning 'beast foot' in Greek. They walked on their back legs, with their heads held out in front and their long tails used for balance. This meant they were quick and nimble, such as **eoraptor** which was useful for catching tiny animals.

Eoraptors lived at the same time as the dicynodonts, a group of herbivorous reptiles that thrived in the Triassic period. They were built like tanks. Some were as big as oxen, some as small as rats; maybe eoraptor would have tried its luck with a rat-sized dicynodont.

Eoraptor

What makes a theropod?

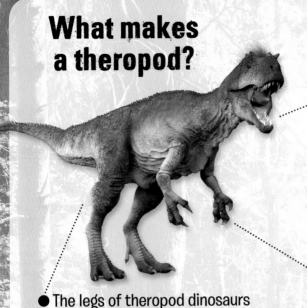

● Theropod teeth were sharp, curved backwards and serrated like a steak knife, perfect for trapping and munching through prey.

● The legs of theropod dinosaurs extended down from the body, unlike reptiles, which usually grew out at the side. Vertical limbs can support a greater weight than sprawling limbs. This helped dinosaurs to grow so large.

● Theropods, walked on two legs. They had three main fingers on their hands, usually with sharp claws. The fourth and fifth digits were much smaller.

Dicynodont

EORAPTOR
Location: South America
Length: 1 metre (39in)

| Precambrian 4,540-541mya |
| Cambrian 541-485 mya |
| Ordovician 485-443 mya |
| Silurian 443-419 mya |
| Devonian 419-359 mya |
| Carboniferous 359-299 mya |
| Permian 299-252 mya |

Triassic 252-201 mya

| Jurassic 201-145 mya |
| Cretaceous 145-66 mya |
| Paleogene 66-23 mya |
| Neogene 23-2.6 mya |
| Quaternary 2.6 mya - present |

Did You Know?
During the middle Triassic period, rauisuchians (raw-i-sook-key-ans) were the top predators. They were not dinosaurs, but reptiles closely related to crocodiles. The largest were about 7 metres (23ft) long.

33

REACH FOR THE SKY

Eudimorphodon, a type of pterosaur, was neither a bird nor a bat, but a reptile that evolved a layer of skin and muscle stretching from the fourth finger of its arm down to its ankles. It must have been like having a tough cape attached to your body! By flapping its arms, it could lift itself off the ground.

Why did it need to fly?

Well, that way it could escape predators and find new habitats for nesting. Being able to fly would have also helped it to catch new types of prey, such as flying insects.

The pterosaurs of the sky lasted as long as the dinosaurs on land, from around 230 to 66 million years ago, when a mass extinction occurred. And just like the dinosaurs, the pterosaurs got bigger and bigger during this time. The first ones were the size of paper planes, but by the end of the Cretaceous period some were as massive as fighter jets!

As pterosaurs grew larger, they got better at flying. Their arms became longer and their wings more blade-like and aerodynamic. They had one problem, though: as they grew bigger, they needed stronger limbs to get off the ground. Thicker bones would have helped, but they would have been too heavy. The answer? Hollow bones, with walls no thicker than a playing card and struts inside for support. Many animals, including dinosaurs, had some hollow bones. However, pterosaurs had many throughout their body, not just in their arms, but also in their pelvis, ribs and vertebrae.

The first pterosaur fossil was found in 1784 in Bavaria, Germany, by the Italian naturalist Cosimo Alessandro Collini. Unfortunately, Collini made one big mistake when he studied his fossil: he thought he was looking at a sea creature with flippers, not a pterosaur with wings.

EUDIMORPHODON
Location: Western Europe
Length: 60cm (2ft)

Eudimorphodon

Precambrian	4,540-541 mya
Cambrian	541-485 mya
Ordovician	485-443 mya
Silurian	443-419 mya
Devonian	419-359 mya
Carboniferous	359-299 mya
Permian	299-252 mya
Triassic	252-201 mya
Jurassic	201-145 mya
Cretaceous	145-66 mya
Paleogene	66-23 mya
Neogene	23-2.6 mya
Quaternary	2.6 mya - present

Did You Know?

Apart from insects, pterosaurs were the first animals to fly, and probably evolved from a small gliding ancestor.

35

BEATING AROUND THE BUSH

Prosauropods were the first dinosaurs to feed only on vegetation, and the first animals tall enough to feed on high vegetation. All herbivores before them had been squat, short-necked animals.

Before you say anything, I know I'm a squat, short-necked animal –

but I ate fish, thank you very much!

Scientists can learn a lot from plant as well as animal fossils. Glossopteris was a tree about 3.5 metres (12ft) tall, with tongue-shaped leaves, that evolved about 300 million years ago. Its fossils have been found in India, South America, Africa, Australia and Antarctica. This led Austrian geologist Eduard Suess to realize that all these regions must have been part of the same land mass we now call Pangaea (see page 7).

Plateosaurus

Most dinosaurs are known from a handful of fossils, but palaeontologists have found over 100 **Plateosaurus** skeletons across Europe. Because many were found in the same places, scientists think Plateosaurus must have roamed in herds. They probably travelled across the dry European landscape of the late Triassic period looking for places with water and plant life.

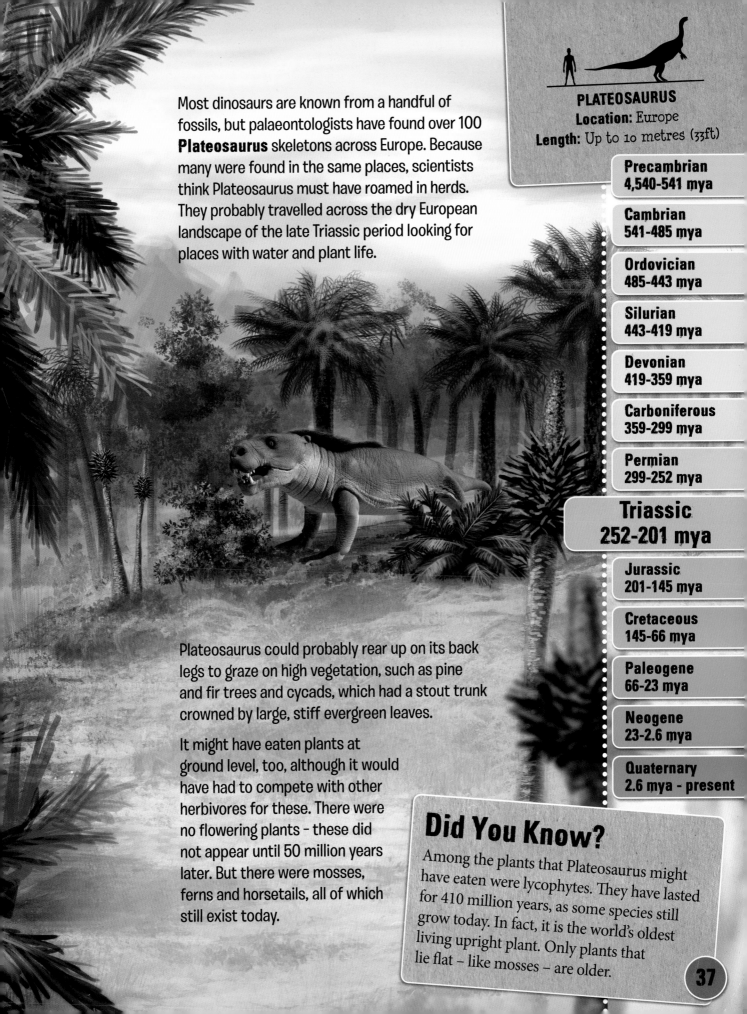

PLATEOSAURUS
Location: Europe
Length: Up to 10 metres (33ft)

Precambrian	4,540-541 mya
Cambrian	541-485 mya
Ordovician	485-443 mya
Silurian	443-419 mya
Devonian	419-359 mya
Carboniferous	359-299 mya
Permian	299-252 mya
Triassic	**252-201 mya**
Jurassic	201-145 mya
Cretaceous	145-66 mya
Paleogene	66-23 mya
Neogene	23-2.6 mya
Quaternary	2.6 mya - present

Plateosaurus could probably rear up on its back legs to graze on high vegetation, such as pine and fir trees and cycads, which had a stout trunk crowned by large, stiff evergreen leaves.

It might have eaten plants at ground level, too, although it would have had to compete with other herbivores for these. There were no flowering plants - these did not appear until 50 million years later. But there were mosses, ferns and horsetails, all of which still exist today.

Did You Know?

Among the plants that Plateosaurus might have eaten were lycophytes. They have lasted for 410 million years, as some species still grow today. In fact, it is the world's oldest living upright plant. Only plants that lie flat – like mosses – are older.

MEAT-EATING MONSTERS

Desmatosuchus was a type of reptile known as an aetosaur, meaning 'eagle lizard'. It was called this because its skull resembled a bird's. But attached to its bird-like skull were a pig-like snout and a crocodile-like body – what a crazy mix! Oh, and it was covered in plating like an armadillo. It needed a suit of armour and shoulder spikes to survive an attack.

At the end of the Triassic period, meat-eating dinosaurs became the top predators in North and South America. They grew up to 7 metres (23ft) long and would pounce on their prey with their powerful hind legs before finishing off their victims with their sharp teeth and ripping claws.

Today's victim is Desmatosuchus.

It might look frightening – especially with those big spikes on its shoulders – but it was actually a big softie. Desmatosuchus had small peg-like teeth that indicate it probably ate soft plants that it uprooted with its shovel-like snout.

American palaeontologist Kenneth Carpenter was born in 1949 in Japan, where he grew up. His favourite film as a boy was *Godzilla*, about a great monster that ravaged Tokyo. In 1997 in New Mexico, USA, he found the first skeleton of a fearsome new dinosaur, and called it **Gojirasaurus**, combining 'Gojira', Japanese for Godzilla, with 'saurus', Greek for lizard.

Gojirasaurus

Desmatosuchus

GOJIRASAURUS
Location: North America
Length: 6 metres (20ft)

Precambrian 4,540-541 mya

Cambrian 541-485 mya

Ordovician 485-443 mya

Silurian 443-419 mya

Devonian 419-359 mya

Carboniferous 359-299 mya

Permian 299-252 mya

Triassic 252-201 mya

Jurassic 201-145 mya

Cretaceous 145-66 mya

Paleogene 66-23 mya

Neogene 23-2.6 mya

Quaternary 2.6 mya - present

At the end of the Triassic period, a mass extinction occurred. Scientists are not sure what caused it - perhaps volcanic eruptions or an asteroid impact. But it wiped out about three-quarters of the Earth's species and started the break-up of Pangaea (see page 7).

Did You Know?

The full name of the species is *Gojirasaurus quayi*. The word *quayi* comes from Quay County, New Mexico, where Kenneth Carpenter discovered the dinosaur.

BATTLE OF THE BIG BEASTS

Believe it or not, two of the biggest beasts of the late Jurassic period went toe-to-toe in epic fights. We know this because the neck of one **Stegosaurus** fossil shows a U-shaped wound that matches the jaws of an **Allosaurus**. And an Allosaurus fossil has a wound in the tail that matches a Stegosaurus tail spike.

Stegosaurus

Allosaurus

Stegosaurus would have had its work cut out against Allosaurus, the top predator of the time. Some scientists think that, when it was threatened, blood rushed to the plates on its back to signal an angry red warning. If this didn't put a predator off, Stegosaurus would have lashed out with its spiked tail. And those spikes could do some damage - they were up to 1 metre (39in) long.

STEGOSAURUS
Location: North America; Western Europe
Length: Up to 9 metres (30ft)

In 1991, scientists found an almost complete skeleton of an Allosaurus in Wyoming, USA. They called him 'Big Al', even though he was six years old when he died and had not quite reached adult size: up to 12 metres (40ft) long.

Big Al's skeleton shows he had suffered 11 broken bones. The first, in his tail, was caused by a fall, perhaps after he had been hit by a Stegosaurus tail! He also had broken ribs, probably from fighting another Allosaurus.

His final injury, a broken toe, stopped him getting to water. His skeleton was found with the head and tail pulled up into an arc. This was a sign that his body had dried out in the sun, suggesting there wasn't much water around.

Allosaurus was one big, mean fighting machine.

Its teeth were about 10cm (4in) long, razor sharp and growing all the time, ready to replace old and lost ones. Some scientists even think it attacked with an open mouth, using its jaws like a hatchet to hack into its victim's flesh.

But surely even a creature as savage as Allosaurus wouldn't take on Stegosaurus? After all, Stegosaurus was built like a tank and had that fearsome spiked tail for protection...

| Precambrian 4,540-541 mya |
| Cambrian 541-485 mya |
| Ordovician 485-443 mya |
| Silurian 443-419 mya |
| Devonian 419-359 mya |
| Carboniferous 359-299 mya |
| Permian 299-252 mya |
| Triassic 252-201 mya |
| **Jurassic 201-145 mya** |
| Cretaceous 145-66 mya |
| Paleogene 66-23 mya |
| Neogene 23-2.6 mya |
| Quaternary 2.6 mya - present |

Did You Know?

The spiked tail of stegosaurs is known as a thagomizer. This name was coined as a joke in 1982 by cartoonist Gary Larson in his comic strip, *The Far Side* – but soon the word was also being used by scientists.

GENTLE GIANTS

Hey, if you think elephants are huge, you should check out the sauropods. They were massive plant-eating dinosaurs that probably evolved from a prosauropod ancestor in the middle of the Jurassic period.

To me, they look like walking whales.

They had big bodies with ridiculously long necks and tails, but their heads were tiny with small brains – clever enough, though, to survive in their environment.

Scientists used to think sauropods, such as **Diplodocus**, evolved their long necks to reach the highest leaves in the trees. This idea makes perfect sense. Like today's giraffes, they would have had their own private food supply, out of reach of all the herbivorous animals at ground level, and been able to spot sources of food or threats from predators at a distance.

However, there is a problem. How did a sauropod's heart pump blood to heights of over 10 metres (33ft)? One expert estimated that it would have had to weigh 1,450kg (1.6 tons)! So he suggested that sauropods had extra hearts in their necks to help the process.

Diplodocus

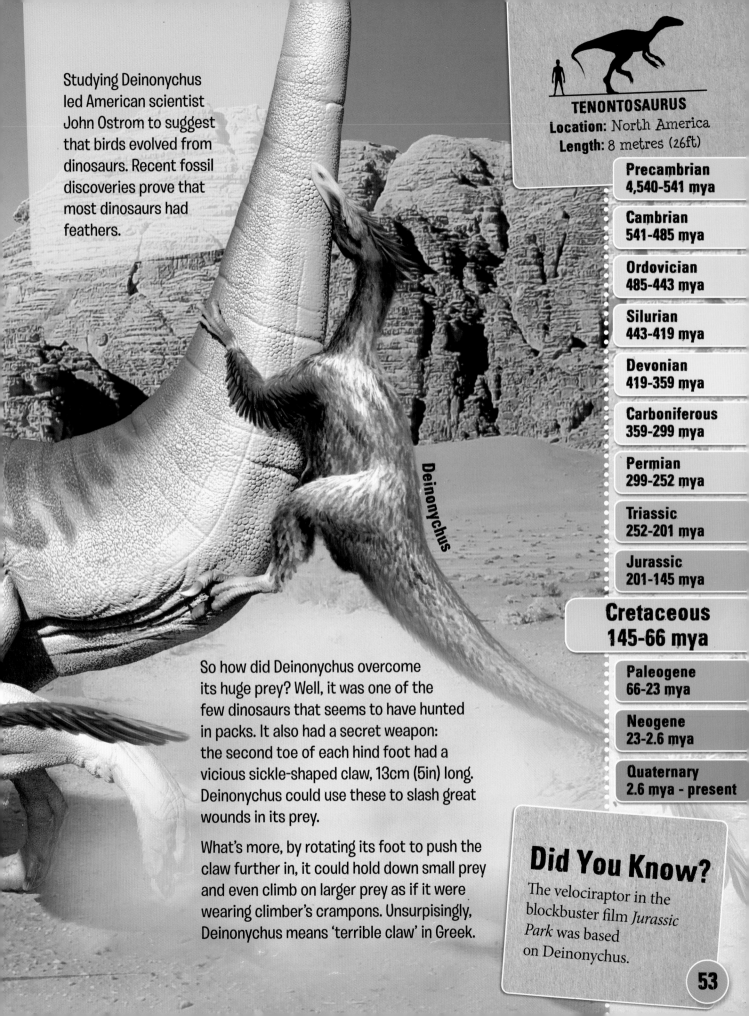

Studying Deinonychus led American scientist John Ostrom to suggest that birds evolved from dinosaurs. Recent fossil discoveries prove that most dinosaurs had feathers.

Deinonychus

So how did Deinonychus overcome its huge prey? Well, it was one of the few dinosaurs that seems to have hunted in packs. It also had a secret weapon: the second toe of each hind foot had a vicious sickle-shaped claw, 13cm (5in) long. Deinonychus could use these to slash great wounds in its prey.

What's more, by rotating its foot to push the claw further in, it could hold down small prey and even climb on larger prey as if it were wearing climber's crampons. Unsurprisingly, Deinonychus means 'terrible claw' in Greek.

Did You Know?

The velociraptor in the blockbuster film *Jurassic Park* was based on Deinonychus.

BIG BEASTS

Diplodocus was the longest dinosaur, at 30 metres (98ft) in length, but it looked like a lightweight next to Dreadnoughtus.

22m

In 2014, scientists announced the discovery of the biggest dinosaur ever to have roamed the Earth. They called it **Dreadnoughtus**, after a fearsome World War I battleship. 'Dreadnought' is from early English and means 'fear nothing'.

20m

18m

The specimen was found in 2005 in Patagonia, Argentina. As the find was in a remote region and the bones were so big, it took four years to excavate the remains.

16m

14m

Then it took palaeontologists five years to study the bones, reconstruct them into one skeleton and publish the results of their findings.

The specimen was 26 metres (85ft) long, including an 11-metre (37-ft) neck and 9-metre (30-ft) tail. And get this, it wasn't even a fully grown adult! Scientists knew this because its shoulder bones had not yet fused together, which would have happened in an adult of its type.

12m

Check out that monster in the middle. It's the sauropod dinosaur Dreadnoughtus and it weighed about 60,000kg (66 tons) – or, to put it another way, the equivalent of twelve African elephants, seven T. rexes, two and a half Diplodocuses or one Boeing 737 (with passengers and baggage on board)!

8m

Here you can see how it shapes up against **Giganotosaurus** and another sauropod, **Diplodocus**. Scientists think Giganotosaurus, which also lived in Argentina, was the second biggest meat-eating dinosaur ever. The biggest meat-eater?

6m

4m

See pages 50–51 to find this out.

And no, it's not T. rex.

2m

Diplodocus

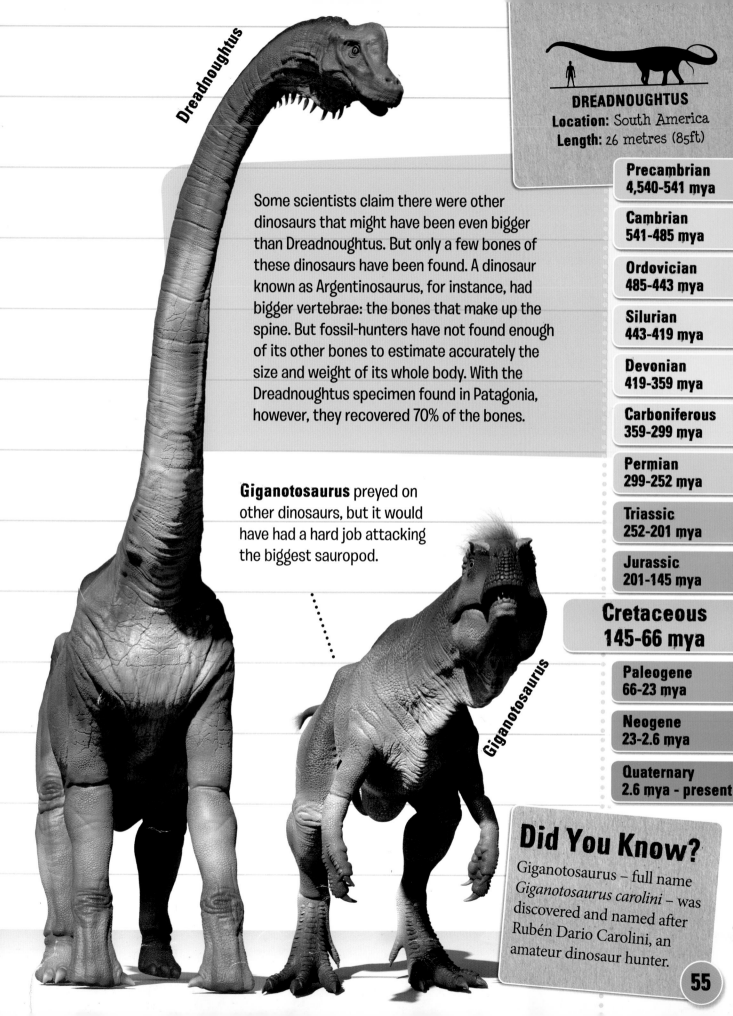

Dreadnoughtus

Some scientists claim there were other dinosaurs that might have been even bigger than Dreadnoughtus. But only a few bones of these dinosaurs have been found. A dinosaur known as Argentinosaurus, for instance, had bigger vertebrae: the bones that make up the spine. But fossil-hunters have not found enough of its other bones to estimate accurately the size and weight of its whole body. With the Dreadnoughtus specimen found in Patagonia, however, they recovered 70% of the bones.

Giganotosaurus preyed on other dinosaurs, but it would have had a hard job attacking the biggest sauropod.

Giganotosaurus

DREADNOUGHTUS
Location: South America
Length: 26 metres (85ft)

| Precambrian 4,540-541 mya |
| Cambrian 541-485 mya |
| Ordovician 485-443 mya |
| Silurian 443-419 mya |
| Devonian 419-359 mya |
| Carboniferous 359-299 mya |
| Permian 299-252 mya |
| Triassic 252-201 mya |
| Jurassic 201-145 mya |
| **Cretaceous 145-66 mya** |
| Paleogene 66-23 mya |
| Neogene 23-2.6 mya |
| Quaternary 2.6 mya - present |

Did You Know?

Giganotosaurus – full name *Giganotosaurus carolini* – was discovered and named after Rubén Dario Carolini, an amateur dinosaur hunter.

55

PREHISTORIC HANG GLIDERS

Imagine a creature as tall as a giraffe when on the ground, and with the wingspan of a fighter jet when in the air. Meet **Quetzalcoatlus**, the largest flying creature that ever existed.

Quetzalcoatlus was a type of flying reptile known as a pterosaur. Pterosaurs emerged about 230 million years ago, at the same time as the dinosaurs. And just like dinosaurs, as the pterosaurs evolved,

they got bigger and bigger...

Quetzalcoatlus may have been lord of the skies 70 million years ago, but today nobody is quite sure how this enormous creature managed to get off the ground in the first place. Some scientists think it needed a cliff to jump off, or at least a downward slope to act as a runway. Others suggest it may have lost the ability to fly and adapted to living on land, like the modern ostrich.

What Quetzalcoatlus ate is a mystery, too. Some believe it flew down to water and skimmed fish into its 1-metre-long (39-in) beak – yet it lived hundreds of kilometres from the seas. Others think its long, thin beak would have been perfect for poking deep inside carcasses - so maybe, like the vulture, it lived by scavenging. Or, perhaps like the modern storks, it simply stalked small animals on land.

Quetzalcoatlus

QUETZALCOATLUS
Location: North America
Wingspan: 10-11 metres (33-36ft)

Precambrian
4,540-541 mya

Cambrian
541-485 mya

Ordovician
485-443 mya

Silurian
443-419 mya

Devonian
419-359 mya

Carboniferous
359-299 mya

Permian
299-252 mya

Triassic
252-201 mya

Jurassic
201-145 mya

**Cretaceous
145-66 mya**

Paleogene
66-23 mya

Neogene
23-2.6 mya

Quaternary
2.6 mya - present

Like other pterosaurs, Quetzalcoatlus walked on all fours on land, so would have been able to stalk its prey. And maybe those gigantic wings came in handy for gathering up the prey. It might also have waded through shallow water, picking up fish, snails and shellfish in its giant beak. Although it did not have big feet, it may have had webbing between the toes to help spread its weight on sandy and muddy ground when walking.

Did You Know?
One study says this celestial monarch flew at speeds of up to 130 km/h (80 mph) for seven to 10 days non-stop, and at altitudes of 4,750 metres (15,000 ft). Imagine that passing overhead!

CHILD'S PLAY

Unlike mammals, most reptiles wouldn't exactly win any Best Parenting Awards. They generally abandon their eggs after they have laid them. There are exceptions, of course. In your world, a few lizards and snakes guard their eggs: pythons incubate their eggs for a while, and crocodiles tend both the eggs and the hatchlings. But, check out this vegetarian **Maiasaura** –

she really did show the love.

In the 1970s, more than 200 specimens of Maiasaura were found in what is now known as Egg Mountain formation, in western Montana, USA. The area was a nesting colony that these dinosaurs returned to year after year. They showed that Maiasaura really cared for their kids.

At the colony, each mother would scrape out a nest in the ground and lay about 20 grapefruit-sized eggs. She didn't sit on the eggs to keep them warm, but brought rotting vegetation to cover them. As the nests were about 7 metres (23ft) apart,

she could easily walk around without crushing the eggs.

The babies would be about 40cm (16in) when they hatched, and for the first months the mother would bring them plant shoots, leaves and berries to eat. They soon grew from the size of a toaster to the size of a tank.

Maiasaura babies

Maiasaura

MAIASAURA
Location: North America
Length: About 9 metres (30ft)

Precambrian
4,540-541 mya

Cambrian
541-485 mya

Ordovician
485-443 mya

Silurian
443-419 mya

Devonian
419-359 mya

Carboniferous
359-299 mya

Permian
299-252 mya

Triassic
252-201 mya

Jurassic
201-145 mya

Cretaceous
145-66 mya

Paleogene
66-23 mya

Neogene
23-2.6 mya

Quaternary
2.6 mya - present

Maiasaura travelled in herds and scientists think they came back to the same safe place to nest every year. The nesting colony would have allowed them to protect their eggs and babies from predators, such as large lizards and meat-eating dinosaurs. And once they were big enough to leave the nest, the young would be protected as part of the herd.

IS IT A BIRD OR A DINOSAUR?

Protoceratops was quite vulnerable to predators. It had no armour and no horns, while the neck frill at the back of its skull was pretty frail. In fact, the frill was probably used to impress females rather than for protection. This makes some scientists think that Protoceratops only dared come out at night. They point out that it had large eyes, which would have helped it to

see in the dark.

Other scientists believe it came out during the day, but only for short intervals.

Oviraptor

Oviraptor was a small, bird-like dinosaur that lived in Asia about 80 million years ago. Like birds, it had a toothless beak and rigid ribcage, and was covered in feathers. No one knows for sure what it lived on, but the shape of its beak suggests that it ate molluscs (for example, snails) and crustaceans (such as crabs, lobsters and crayfish). Perhaps it also used its sharp beak to shred plants and break open fruit and nuts.

PROTOCERATOPS
Location: Asia
Length: 1.8 metres (6ft)

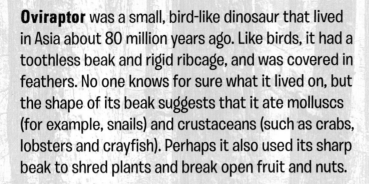

Protoceratops

The name 'Oviraptor' is Latin for 'egg taker' or 'egg seizer'. It was given this name because the first Oviraptor remains were found on top of a clutch of eggs that scientists thought belonged to Protoceratops, a herbivorous dinosaur. The American scientist Henry Fairfield Osborn believed the Oviraptor was trying to steal the eggs. In fact, scientists now think it was brooding a clutch of its own eggs in its nest. Instead of being an egg stealer, it was an egg protector!

| Precambrian 4,540-541 mya |
| Cambrian 541-485 mya |
| Ordovician 485-443 mya |
| Silurian 443-419 mya |
| Devonian 419-359 mya |
| Carboniferous 359-299 mya |
| Permian 299-252 mya |
| Triassic 252-201 mya |
| Jurassic 201-145 mya |

Cretaceous 145-66 mya

| Paleogene 66-23 mya |
| Neogene 23-2.6 mya |
| Quaternary 2.6 mya - present |

Did You Know?

A Protoceratops fossil being prepared for display in Poland in 2011 was found to have its footprint preserved in the rocks encasing the fossilized bones. Scientists think this is the only time one dinosaur's footprint and fossil have been found together.

MASS MOVEMENT

A few hundred years ago, bison used to migrate across North America in huge herds. But 75 million years before this, **Centrosaurus** moved across the continent looking for the best plants to eat. They were bigger than bison and they travelled in herds of around 1,000 animals.

Just imagine it...

whirling clouds of dust and the drumbeat of thousands and thousands of feet. It must have sounded like an earthquake and I reckon it would have frightened the fiercest meat-eating dinosaur.

Centrosaurus

In Alberta, Canada, entire Centrosaurus herds, ranging from youngsters to old adults, have been found together in gigantic graves known as bone-beds. Scientists think many of these mass graves resulted from herds trying to cross flooded rivers. However, at one site, which contains no fewer than 14 mass graves, scientists think a huge hurricane must have blown in from the sea.

You can picture it: the skies darkening, the breeze picking up... and then suddenly, relentless rain, gale-force winds and seawater surging onto the land. As the waters rose, birds flew away, and small mammals and reptiles scurried up trees, and even took their chances at swimming. But slow, dim-witted centrosaurus would probably not have noticed until it was too late. Anyway, where could they escape to in the flat Canadian landscape?

CENTROSAURUS
Location: North America
Length: About 5 metres (20ft)

| Precambrian 4,540-541 mya |
| Cambrian 541-485 mya |
| Ordovician 485-443 mya |
| Silurian 443-419 mya |
| Devonian 419-359 mya |
| Carboniferous 359-299 mya |
| Permian 299-252 mya |
| Triassic 252-201 mya |
| Jurassic 201-145 mya |
| **Cretaceous 145-66 mya** |
| Paleogene 66-23 mya |
| Neogene 23-2.6 mya |
| Quaternary 2.6 mya - present |

Centrosaurus had many relatives in the centrosaurine family, all with different frills and horns on their skulls. Scientists think they all stayed with their own species, much like some of the different herds of grass-eaters on the African continent today. Impala, springbok and kudu, for example, all keep to their own species. By moving in herds, the animals can warn each other of danger and lessen their chances of being singled out by a predator.

Did You Know?
The name Centrosaurus means 'pointed lizard' in Greek, and refers to the small horns on the edge of its frills, not to the front horn (which was unknown when the dinosaur was named).

ARMOURED DINOSAURS

There were many huge, meat-eating dinosaurs in North America in the late Cretaceous period, including the king of dinosaurs, Tyrannosaurus rex. But they needed to choose their prey carefully. Some of the plant-eating dinosaurs evolved defensive armour – and some, like **Ankylosaurus**, could even fight back with a secret weapon.

Game on!

Ankylosaurus was essentially a prehistoric tank: 7 metres (23ft) long, heavily armoured and equipped with a lethal weapon. If a predator was not put off by those threatening spikes, it would soon wreck its teeth on the bite-proof bony plates that covered Ankylosaurus's head, neck, back and tail.

Ankylosaurus

The only place to attack Ankylosaurus was its soft underbelly. However, the creature weighed up to 7,000kg (7.7 tons) and stood very low to the ground, so it would have been impossible to flip it over - even a T. rex couldn't have managed it. And any predator had better watch out, because Ankylosaurus could swipe its tail viciously. This had a hard club at the end that was easily capable of breaking bones.

Styracosaurus (in the background here) was just as scary. It had a huge frill extending from its head, topped with a series of dangerous-looking spikes. Just for good measure, it also had a 60-cm (2-ft) spike on top of its snout. No one would like to be on the receiving end of that.

ANKYLOSAURUS
Location: North America
Length: 7 metres (23ft)

Ankylosaurus had a very small brain, not much bigger than a lime or lemon. Probably only Stegosaurus, the least intelligent of all the dinosaurs, had less grey matter. But, Ankylosaurus didn't need a high IQ. All it had to do was munch on plants - and squat low and swing its tail if any predator made the mistake of attacking it.

Styracosaurus

| Precambrian 4,540-541 mya |
| Cambrian 541-485 mya |
| Ordovician 485-443 mya |
| Silurian 443-419 mya |
| Devonian 419-359 mya |
| Carboniferous 359-299 mya |
| Permian 299-252 mya |
| Triassic 252-201 mya |
| Jurassic 201-145 mya |
| **Cretaceous 145-66 mya** |
| Paleogene 66-23 mya |
| Neogene 23-2.6 mya |
| Quaternary 2.6 mya - present |

Did You Know?

Some scientists think Styracosaurus used to knock down trees with its horns, beak and great weight, then eat the leaves and twigs.

KING OF THE DINOSAURS

Check out this battle between two **Tyrannosaurus rex**. You might think they would have picked on smaller animals. But several T. rex bones have been found with teeth wounds that could only have been made by other T. rexes.

So why did T. rex fight?

Well, eliminating a rival T. rex would make it easier to hunt in one area. Or the battle may have been over a mate or a scavenged carcass.

Meet the ultimate bone crusher. Tyrannosaurus rex was the undisputed king of dinosaurs in the late Cretaceous period. It was up to 6 metres (20ft) tall - about as high as a two-storey house.

Its skull was about 1.5 metres (5ft) long, with the jaws extending to about 1 metre (39in). And those jaws had around 60 teeth, up to 30cm (12in) long. Can you imagine teeth bigger than bananas?

In 2012, scientists tried to work out the force of a T. rex's bite. They found that it was almost 12,800lb, the same as 13 concert grand pianos slamming down on its prey. This makes it the hardest-biting land animal ever known. Megalodon, a giant shark that became extinct about 1.5 million years ago, had the hardest bite at 41,000lb. Deinosuchus, a crocodile that lived in North America at the same time as T. rex, also had a more powerful bite, at 23,000lb.

T. rex needed its 30-cm teeth, as scientists estimate that it could bite off 230kg (500lb) of meat. So it's easy to see why it would attack a fellow T. rex – at 7,000kg (7.7 tons), it made for a hearty meal.

When fighting another T. rex, it would have aimed to clamp down on its opponent's neck or jaws. If it had targeted any other part of the body, it would have been left open to counter-attack.

Tyrannosaurus rex

TYRANNOSAURUS REX
Location: North America
Length: About 12.2 metres (40ft)

Precambrian
4,540-541 mya

Cambrian
541-485 mya

Ordovician
485-443 mya

Silurian
443-419 mya

Devonian
419-359 mya

Carboniferous
359-299 mya

Permian
299-252 mya

Triassic
252-201 mya

Jurassic
201-145 mya

Cretaceous
145-66 mya

Paleogene
66-23 mya

Neogene
23-2.6 mya

Quaternary
2.6 mya - present

T. rex wasn't the only cannibal dinosaur. Majungasaurus, which lived in Madagascar 84-70 million years ago, is also known to have eaten its own kind.

Did You Know?

No one is sure why T. rex's arms were so short. They were probably used for grasping its prey. But they were too short to lift any meat to its mouth – its jaws probably did most of the work!

67

ASTEROID ATTACK!

One of the most dramatic mass extinctions on Earth occurred about 66 million years ago, ending the Cretaceous period.

Over three-quarters of the land animals died out

– as well as all the huge flying reptiles, known as pterosaurs, and all the giant sea reptiles, such as pliosaurs and mosasaurs. The only dinosaurs to escape the destruction were those with wings that had evolved into birds.

What's the difference between an asteroid, a meteor and a meteorite? An asteroid is a rocky object in space that orbits the sun. Sometimes asteroids enter the Earth's atmosphere and then they are known as meteors. They burn and vaporize, leaving bright streaks in the sky, so meteors are also known as 'shooting stars'. If a meteor survives the plunge through the atmosphere and lands on the Earth, it's known as a meteorite.

Scientists estimate that the asteroid created an impact about 2 million times greater than the most powerful nuclear bomb ever detonated. It made a crater measuring 180km (110 miles) wide.

Turtles and crocodiles survived the end-Cretaceous extinction, along with smaller animals such as snails, snakes, amphibians - including salamanders and frogs - and small lizards, such as iguanas.

| Precambrian 4,540-541 mya |
| Cambrian 541-485 mya |
| Ordovician 485-443 mya |
| Silurian 443-419 mya |
| Devonian 419-359 mya |
| Carboniferous 359-299 mya |
| Permian 299-252 mya |
| Triassic 252-201 mya |
| Jurassic 201-145 mya |
| **Cretaceous 145-66 mya** |
| Paleogene 66-23 mya |
| Neogene 23-2.6 mya |
| Quaternary 2.6 mya - present |

Dinosaurs had been alive for a staggering 165 million years. So why did they suddenly die out? In 1980, the American scientist Luis Alvarez came up with an answer. He found that rock from the end of the Cretaceous period contained lots of iridium, a metal that is rare on Earth but common in asteroids. This led him to believe that a massive asteroid must have hit the Earth and wiped out the dinosaurs.

The problem? An asteroid would have left a huge crater somewhere. An answer came when scientists found the

Chicxulub (cheek-she-loob) crater on the seabed near Mexico (see above). It had been created by a meteorite 10km (6 miles) wide that threw masses of super-hot dust into the Earth's atmosphere, blocking out the sun.

Without sunlight, many plants died, so the herbivorous dinosaurs had nothing to eat. And without the herbivores, the carnivorous dinosaurs had nothing to eat. The era of the dinosaurs was over.

Did You Know?

The end-Cretaceous extinction was not the only mass extinction in the history of the Earth. There have been five, with the worst at the end of the Permian period, 252 million years ago, when about 95% of all species died out. Scientists think this was caused by huge volcanic eruptions that lasted 600,000 years!

AMAZING MAMMALS

Mammals, like reptiles and amphibians, are tetrapods (four-limbed). And you know who was the first tetrapod?

Yes, that's right, you're looking at him.

You, *Homo sapiens*, evolved from the likes of me. Mind you, we've had to wait a long time for you to arrive. I grew limbs and pulled myself onto the riverbank about 365 million years ago. The first mammals came into existence about 210 million years ago, and *Homo sapiens* arose as a recognizable species about 200,000 years ago.

Mammals actually lived alongside dinosaurs for about 145 million years, but they kept a pretty low profile. Most were the size of mice and only ventured out at night. After the dinosaurs were wiped out about 66 million years ago, life became less scary for mammals and they began to eat a variety of foods and explore new places to live.

Some mammals, such as the primate **Smilodectes** (above right), started to climb trees. Others, such as bats and **Planetetherium** (right), developed wings to glide or fly. And muscular **Stylinodon** was an efficient digger that probably ate roots and tubers. Some mammals even returned to the water (see pages 80-81).

Stylinodon

Smilodectes

Planetetherium

Precambrian
4,540–541 mya

Cambrian
541–485 mya

Ordovician
485–443 mya

Silurian
443–419 mya

Devonian
419–359 mya

Carboniferous
359–299 mya

Permian
299–252 mya

Triassic
252–201 mya

Jurassic
201–145 mya

Cretaceous
145–66 mya

**Paleogene
66–23 mya**

Neogene
23–2.6 mya

Quaternary
2.6 mya – present

These mammals all lived in North America from 56 to 45 million years ago.

Humans are primates. One of the first primates was Notharctus. It was tiny but had some features similar to human beings, including a relatively flat face instead of a snout, flexible hands that could grab branches, and a big brain relative to its body size.

Did You Know?

The largest mammal ever is the present-day blue whale. It can weigh up to 200 tonnes (440,000lb) and measure up to 30 metres (100ft). The smallest – Kitti's hog-nosed bat – is about 3cm (1.2in) in length and weighs a mere 2g (0.07oz). It lives in caves in Burma and Thailand and is an endangered species. As it is so small, it is often called the bumblebee bat.

71

MEET THE MEAT-EATERS

The earliest dog was **Hesperocyon**, which lived in North America 40 to 35 million years ago. It was about the size of a small fox and may have lived in packs, either in trees or in underground burrows. The first cat, Proailurus, appeared in Europe and Asia about 30 to 25 million years ago.

Unlike **creodonts** (far right), cats and dogs were good hunters. They were fast, powerful and cunning, and had excellent eyesight, hearing and sense of smell.

Hesperocyon's most dog-like feature was its ears.

Smilodon was a type of sabre-toothed cat. It roamed across North and South America as late as 10,000 years ago.

Hesperocyon

Smilodon

Cats and dogs evolved different ways of hunting. Dogs and their close relatives, wolves, usually formed packs to chase their prey until it was exhausted. Big cats sometimes lived in groups but were stealthier hunters: they quietly crept up on their prey, then pounced.

Around 60 million years ago, some mammals started hunting other mammals. Among the first to do so were Creodonts. They lived from 55 to 35 million years ago and had teeth that could slice up flesh like scissors.

This made eating other animals easy!

However, they were slow, had small brains and were not able to turn their wrists inwards to trip, slash or grab prey.

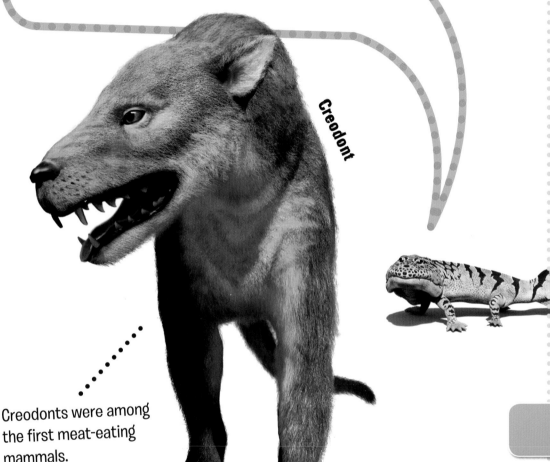

Creodont

Creodonts were among the first meat-eating mammals.

Precambrian 4,540-541 mya	
Cambrian 541-485 mya	
Ordovician 485-443 mya	
Silurian 443-419 mya	
Devonian 419-359 mya	
Carboniferous 359-299 mya	
Permian 299-252 mya	
Triassic 252-201 mya	
Jurassic 201-145 mya	
Cretaceous 145-66 mya	
Paleogene 66-23 mya	
Neogene 23-2.6 mya	
Quaternary 2.6 mya - present	

Smilodon had a very effective way of killing prey. Its magnificent canines were 30cm (12in) long, but its teeth broke easily and its jaws were weak, so it couldn't risk a fight.

Scientists think it pounced on its prey from the branches of trees, sank its canines into the neck of its victim, then quickly completed the kill with its powerful forelimbs.

A WHALE OF A TIME

The name of the monster shark **Megalodon** means 'giant tooth' in Greek. Check out one of its teeth and you'll see why. It is razor sharp, serrated and 18cm (7in) long. Compare that to the teeth of the great white shark of your time: a paltry 3cm (1.2in) long.

But it wasn't just the size of its teeth that made Megalodon so fearsome – it was the force with which it used them. In 2012, scientists estimated its bite force was over three times greater than T. rex's and almost 50 times greater than a lion's.

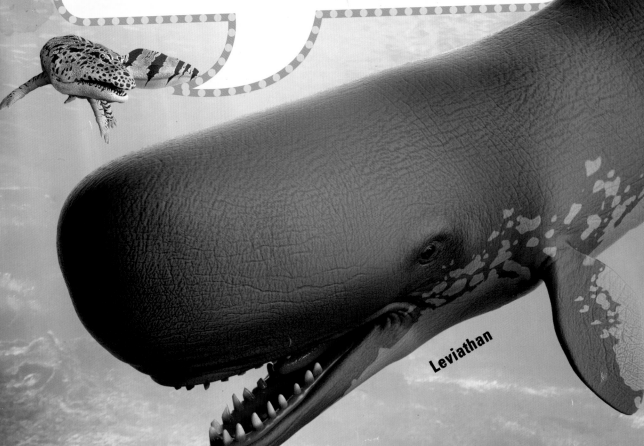

Leviathan

Megalodon lived from about 16 to 2.6 million years ago. As it was the size of a bus, it would have needed some sizeable dinners. The giant turtle Stupendemys might have made a tasty starter. Its shell measured about 3 x 2 metres (10 x 6ft), but for Megalodon it would have been like crunching a potato crisp.

For the main course, Megalodon would surely have been looking for a nice fat whale. We know it attacked whales, because bite marks have been found in many whale fossils, especially in their flipper bones and the vertebrae in the tail fin.

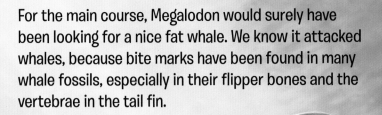

Megalodon

Megalodon might even have targeted **Leviathan**, a vast sperm whale that lived about 12-13 million years ago. This would be risky, though. Livyatan was almost as big as Megalodon and had even bigger teeth, at 36cm (14in). This fight is going to be a gore-fest!

Megalodon teeth have been found in oceans all around the world, so keep your eyes open when you are by the seaside. Some vertebrae - the bones that make up the spine - have also been found. Scientists have to estimate the size of Megalodon from these teeth and vertebrae, because the rest of a shark's skeleton is made up of soft cartilage, which doesn't fossilize well.

MEGALODON
Location: Oceans worldwide
Length: About 16 metres (52ft)

| Precambrian 4,540-541 mya |
| Cambrian 541-485 mya |
| Ordovician 485-443 mya |
| Silurian 443-419 mya |
| Devonian 419-359 mya |
| Carboniferous 359-299 mya |
| Permian 299-252 mya |
| Triassic 252-201 mya |
| Jurassic 201-145 mya |
| Cretaceous 145-66 mya |
| Paleogene 66-23 mya |

Neogene 23-2.6 mya

| Quaternary 2.6 mya - present |

Did You Know?
Scientists think Megalodon might have targeted the fins of a whale first, to immobilize it, before they started feeding on the body.

MONSTROUS MAMMALS

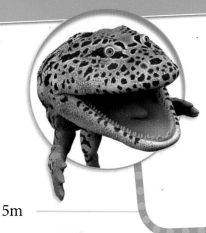

If you think elephants, gorillas and rhinos are big, how about these **super-sized** mammals that once roamed the Earth...

5m

4m

Chalicotherium 25 to about 5 million years ago. The horse is probably the closest modern relative of this 3-metre (10-ft) monster - but this chalicotherium certainly didn't look like many modern steeds. Its front legs were much longer than its hind ones, and instead of hooves it had claws, which it probably used to gather vegetation. Some Scientists think that it brushed the knuckles of its front feet along the ground when it walked - like a modern gorilla.

3m

2m

1m

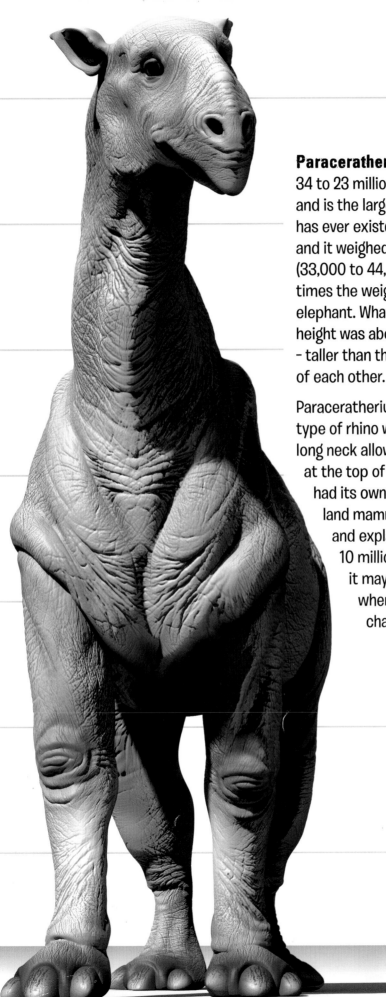

Paraceratherium

34 to 23 million years ago, and is the largest land mammal that has ever existed. It's a Paraceratherium and it weighed about 15-20 tonnes (33,000 to 44,000lb) - about four times the weight of an African elephant. What's more, its shoulder height was about 4.8 metres (15ft 9in) - taller than three adult humans on top of each other.

Paraceratherium lived in Asia and was a type of rhino without a horn. Its extra long neck allowed it to reach leaves at the top of the trees. This meant it had its own food source, as no other land mammal could reach so high and explains why it lived for over 10 million years. Scientists think it may have become extinct when the forests of Asia changed to grasslands.

Precambrian
4,540-541 mya

Cambrian
541-485 mya

Ordovician
485-443 mya

Silurian
443-419 mya

Devonian
419-359 mya

Carboniferous
359-299 mya

Permian
299-252 mya

Triassic
252-201 mya

Jurassic
201-145 mya

Cretaceous
145-66 mya

Paleogene
66-23 mya

Neogene
23-2.6 mya

Quaternary
2.6 mya - present

Did You Know?

Gigantopithecus, a real bigfoot, existed about 100,000 years ago. Scientists have found teeth and jaw bones of this 3-metre (10-ft) ape in Vietnam, China and Nepal.

THE KILLER PIGS

Entelodonts are often called killer pigs - and you can see why. Their jaws and muscles were specially designed for bone crushing. The bones of primitive rhinos, camels and cows have all been found with wounds made by entelodonts. However, scientists can't agree whether these hideous hogs scavenged on dead carcasses - like vultures - or attacked and killed animals, as lions do.

They certainly attacked their own kind. Many entelodont skulls have been found with gashes up to 2cm (0.75in) deep, which can only have been inflicted by other killer pigs. In a fight, it seems to have been quite common for one pig to fit another's head entirely in its mouth! Luckily, like modern warthogs, entelodonts had bony lumps on their skulls protecting their eyes and nose.

Entelodont

Daeodon was one of the largest entelodonts. It lived about 20 million years ago, and had a huge skull about 90cm (3ft) long – that's about the size of a dustbin! The skull also had two extra-wide cheekbones, which anchored its really powerful biting muscles.

ENTELODONT
Location: Asia, Europe, America
Length: Up to 3.5 metres (11ft)

Pigs are pretty harmless creatures, happy to spend their days wallowing in mud and rooting around in the ground for food. Right?

Well, let me introduce you to the entelodonts.

These were no ordinary farmyard pigs. The smallest ones were about twice the size of today's pigs. And the biggest? They were the size of a rhino. And while entelodonts may have been from the same family of mammals as deer, horses, cattle and giraffes, they were certainly no peace-loving vegetarians...

Precambrian	4,540-541 mya
Cambrian	541-485 mya
Ordovician	485-443 mya
Silurian	443-419 mya
Devonian	419-359 mya
Carboniferous	359-299 mya
Permian	299-252 mya
Triassic	252-201 mya
Jurassic	201-145 mya
Cretaceous	145-66 mya

Paleogene
66-23 mya

Neogene
23-2.6 mya

Quaternary
2.6 mya - present

Did You Know?
Like modern-day pigs, entelodonts were probably omnivores, eating both meat and plants. They probably dug up roots and tubers if no meat was available.

79

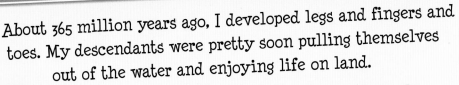

About 365 million years ago, I developed legs and fingers and toes. My descendants were pretty soon pulling themselves out of the water and enjoying life on land.

However, some 315 million years later, mammals – built for life on solid ground – started to evolve back into sea creatures, such as whales.

Why did they do this?

Probably because food was scarce on land and the sea was full of irresistibly tasty treats.

How did whales change?

Whales didn't only lose their limbs and develop a streamlined shape ideal for swimming. Their bodies evolved in lots of other ways...

Blowhole: The 'nose' moved from the face to the top of the head. This meant the whale could breathe while most of its body was underwater.

Lungs: Whales are really good at breathing! In one breath, your body might absorb 15% of the oxygen you inhale. Whales, on the other hand, take in as much as 90%.

Blubber: The depths of the oceans are very cold, because sunlight rarely reaches below 200 metres (656ft). To keep warm, whales developed a layer of fat called blubber, just below the skin.

Pakicetus This wolf-like creature is the earliest known ancestor of the whale. Scientists know this because its earbone was similar to a whale's, and its ankle bone similar to those of hoofed land mammals and cetaceans (the whale group). Pakicetus ate meat but also liked fish, so it evolved features to help it swim after sea creatures.

Ambulocetus Its name means 'walking whale' and it probably swam like modern whales, arching its spine and pushing its tail up and down in the water. Also like whales, it did not have external ears but picked up vibrations through its jawbone. To detect prey on land, it may have lowered its head to the ground and felt for vibrations.

Pakicetus
50 million years ago

Ambulocetus
50-48 million years ago

Kutchicetus 46-43 million years ago. Its long tail helped it move quickly through the water.

Rodhocetus 48-41 million years ago. As with whales, its hip bones were not fused to its backbone, which made swimming easier.

Dorudon 40-30 million years ago. Its nostrils, or blowhole, were on the top of its head and its front legs were paddle-like flippers.

About 30 million years ago, whales divided into two orders:

Toothed whales, or **Odontocetes**, hunt other large sea creatures. To detect prey, they developed echolocation - sending out sound pulses from their foreheads and then sensing the echo of these sounds through the jaws. The toothed whales include all species of dolphin and porpoise.

Baleen whales, or **Mysticetes**, feed on tiny sea creatures and have comb-like baleen plates rather than teeth in their upper jaws. The baleen plates capture shrimp-like krill and other small animals every time the whale takes in a huge mouthful of sea water.

AMBULOCETUS
Location: Shores of Central Asia
Length: About 3 metres (10ft)

| Precambrian 4,540-541 mya |
| Cambrian 541-485 mya |
| Ordovician 485-443 mya |
| Silurian 443-419 mya |
| Devonian 419-359 mya |
| Carboniferous 359-299 mya |
| Permian 299-252 mya |
| Triassic 252-201 mya |
| Jurassic 201-145 mya |
| Cretaceous 145-66 mya |

Paleogene 66-23 mya

Neogene 23-2.6 mya

Quaternary 2.6 mya - present

Did You Know?

The gigantic blue whale is a baleen whale, feeding only on very small sea animals.

TERROR BIRDS

Can you imagine birds much taller than an adult human, with skulls up to 70cm (2ft 4in) long, attached to powerful, hook-tipped beaks? **Terror birds** were the top predators in South America from about 60 million years ago to 2 million years ago.

Terror bird

These birds didn't fly – they ruled the land. They were built like smaller versions of T. rex, with enormous heads, short arms, long, powerful legs and fearsome beaks. Officially they are called phorusrhacids, but that was way too hard to pronounce so everyone called them **terror birds!**

There were many different species of terror bird, but most probably used the hooked tip of their large, heavy, pointed beak to strike at prey.

Scientists think Andalgalornis - a terror bird that lived about 25 million years ago - would have wielded its beak like a hatchet, inflicting deep wounds with quick, stabbing motions. Then it would withdraw to a safe distance as its victim bled to death. Grappling with the prey in a fight might have been the end for Andalgalornis, because its skull was weak.

TERROR BIRD
Location: South America
Length: Up to 2.5 metres (8ft)

| Precambrian 4,540-541 mya |
| Cambrian 541-485 mya |
| Ordovician 485-443 mya |
| Silurian 443-419 mya |
| Devonian 419-359 mya |
| Carboniferous 359-299 mya |
| Permian 299-252 mya |
| Triassic 252-201 mya |
| Jurassic 201-145 mya |
| Cretaceous 145-66 mya |

Paleogene 66-23 mya

Neogene 23-2.6 mya

Quaternary 2.6 mya - present

Terror birds lived in South America before it joined up with North America, and ate grazing animals. Most scientists believe terror birds were extremely nimble, swift predators that could reach speeds of 48 km/h (30 mph).

Did You Know?

Some terror birds may have shaken smaller prey in their beaks, and even thrown their victims to the ground. This would not only kill the prey but also break their bones, making them easier to swallow!

83

MARVELLOUS MARSUPIALS

Diprotodon might be the same shape and size as a rhino but she's a real gentle giant. She's a marsupial, in the same family as kangaroos, koalas and wombats. And like all female marsupials, she has a pouch in which her babies grow. This faces backwards just like a modern-day wombat's – in fact, Diprotodon is sometimes known as the 'giant wombat'.

Today, there are about 235 species of marsupial in Australia and nearby islands, and about 100 species of American marsupial.

The only monotreme (egg-laying) mammals today are the platypus and four species of spiny anteater, all of which live in Australia and New Guinea.

Placental mammals (see right) are the most common mammals, with about 5,000 species, including humans.

Diprotodon

The first mammals appeared about 210 million years ago and gave birth by laying eggs. They are known as monotremes. However, about 125 million years ago, two new types of mammal evolved: marsupials and placentals.

DIPROTODON
Location: Australia
Length: 3 metres (10ft)

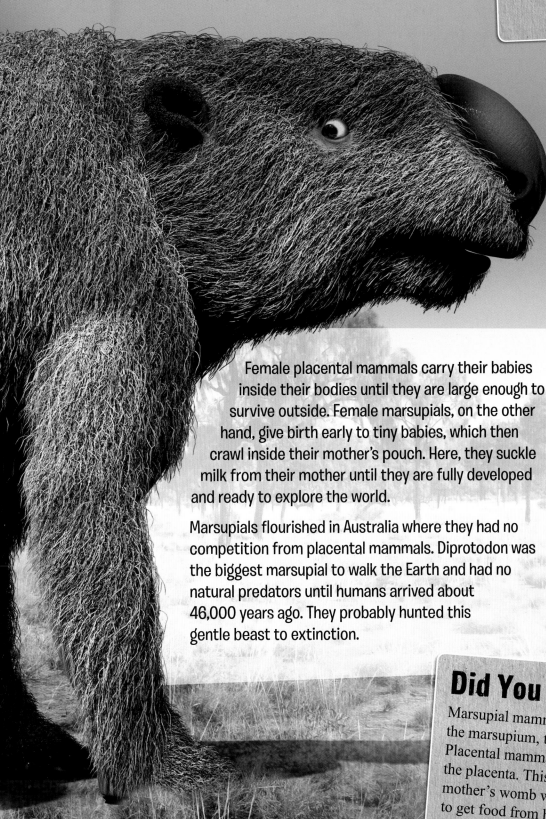

Female placental mammals carry their babies inside their bodies until they are large enough to survive outside. Female marsupials, on the other hand, give birth early to tiny babies, which then crawl inside their mother's pouch. Here, they suckle milk from their mother until they are fully developed and ready to explore the world.

Marsupials flourished in Australia where they had no competition from placental mammals. Diprotodon was the biggest marsupial to walk the Earth and had no natural predators until humans arrived about 46,000 years ago. They probably hunted this gentle beast to extinction.

| Precambrian 4,540-541 mya |
| Cambrian 541-485 mya |
| Ordovician 485-443 mya |
| Silurian 443-419 mya |
| Devonian 419-359 mya |
| Carboniferous 359-299 mya |
| Permian 299-252 mya |
| Triassic 252-201 mya |
| Jurassic 201-145 mya |
| Cretaceous 145-66 mya |
| Paleogene 66-23 mya |
| Neogene 23-2.6 mya |

Quaternary 2.6 mya - present

Did You Know?

Marsupial mammals get their name from the marsupium, the mother's pouch. Placental mammals get their name from the placenta. This is an organ inside the mother's womb which allows babies to get food from her bloodstream.

MONKEY BUSINESS

Around 5 million years ago, two ape-like creatures Ardipithecus and **Australopithecus** did a remarkable thing: they started to walk upright. They still climbed trees with the help of their long arms and long, curved fingers and toes. But when on the ground, they used two feet, not four.

Why did they do this?

Scientists think it was simply to save energy, raise the eyes to see further and free up their forelimbs to carry tools and food.

Australopithecus female

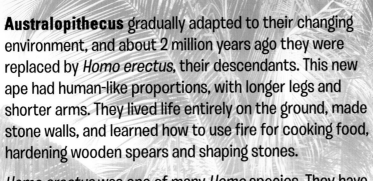

Australopithecus gradually adapted to their changing environment, and about 2 million years ago they were replaced by *Homo erectus*, their descendants. This new ape had human-like proportions, with longer legs and shorter arms. They lived life entirely on the ground, made stone walls, and learned how to use fire for cooking food, hardening wooden spears and shaping stones.

Homo erectus was one of many *Homo* species. They have all died out except one: *Homo sapiens*, better known as humans. We are one of seven existing species in the hominid - or great ape - family. The others are two species of chimpanzee, two species of gorilla and two species of orangutan.

Australopithecus male

Precambrian	4,540-541 mya
Cambrian	541-485 mya
Ordovician	485-443 mya
Silurian	443-419 mya
Devonian	419-359 mya
Carboniferous	359-299 mya
Permian	299-252 mya
Triassic	252-201 mya
Jurassic	201-145 mya
Cretaceous	145-66 mya
Paleogene	66-23 mya
Neogene	**23-2.6 mya**
Quaternary	**2.6 mya - present**

Modern *Homo sapiens* evolved in Africa from about 200,000 to 150,000 years ago. But it was only 70,000 years ago that they started to travel across the world - first to Asia and then, after a bit of island hopping, to Australia. Humans started arriving in Europe about 35,000 years ago and moved into the Americas about 15,000 years ago. They reached New Zealand only about 1,500 years ago, long after the Roman Empire had fallen.

MAGNIFICENT MAMMOTHS

When humans reached Europe about **35,000 years ago**, in the middle of the last Ice Age, they lived side by side with **woolly mammoths**. We know humans hunted these members of the elephant family because several mammoth bones have been found with spear wounds.

Humans didn't hunt woolly mammoths just for their meat. After the feasting was over, they used the pelts for clothing and the bones for constructing homes. Large bones were used for foundations, tusks for entrances and leg bones for walls, while skins were probably stretched over the top to keep the rain out. Any bones left over would have been turned into small sculptures, weapons or fuel for fires. Archaeologists discovered that 149 mammoths had been used to build one settlement at Mezhirich in Ukraine.

Woolly mammoths died out on mainland Europe, Asia and North America about 10,000 years ago. Amazingly, though, some survived on islands: on St Paul Island in Alaska until 6,400 years ago, and on Wrangel Island in the Arctic Ocean until 4,000 years ago.

So how did humans kill these huge creatures? Spears were certainly used. And because many dog and wolf bones have been found with mammoth bones, some experts think humans may have also trained semi-domesticated dogs and wolves to surround a mammoth and immobilize it. Maybe they caught mammoths in pitfall traps, too; there are cave paintings that seem to show this.

WOOLLY MAMMOTH
Location: Plains of North America and Eurasia
Length: About 4 metres (13ft)

Precambrian
4,540-541 mya

Cambrian
541-485 mya

Ordovician
485-443 mya

Silurian
443-419 mya

Devonian
419-359 mya

Carboniferous
359-299 mya

Permian
299-252 mya

Triassic
252-201 mya

Jurassic
201-145 mya

Cretaceous
145-66 mya

Paleogene
66-23 mya

Neogene
23-2.6 mya

Quaternary
2.6 mya - present

Did You Know?

Hunting wasn't the only reason that woolly mammoths died out. The end of the Ice Age, about 10,000 years ago, probably meant the plants they ate stopped growing.

Hallucigenia

Pronounced: Hal-oo-si-gen-ia

For a long time, Hallucigenia was thought to be an 'evolutionary misfit' - in other words, not related to any other animals alive. But in 2014, scientists at Cambridge University suggested it was related to today's velvet worms, which live in tropical forests.

Nautiloid

Pronounced: Nort-ill-oid

Today's nautiloids are sometimes called 'living fossils' because they have changed very little over millions of years. However, only nautiloids with curved shells, not straight ones (as on page 16) have survived.

Dunkleosteus

Pronounced: Dun-kul-oss-tee-us

Dunkleosteus was a type of fish known as a placoderm, which means literally 'plated skin'. Placoderms lasted about 50 million years. Sharks appeared at about the same time but they have survived for over 400 million years.

Arthropleura

Pronounced: Ar-thro-plur-ah

Fossil-hunters have found fossilized footprints of Arthropleura, as well as fossilized body parts. They show that the giant millipede moved quickly across forest floors, swerving to avoid obstacles such as trees and rocks.

Cynodont

Pronounced: Sigh-no-dont

Cynodonts had teeth like those of mammals: they had incisors at the front of the mouth for nipping off food, canines at the sides for piercing flesh, and molars at the back for chewing food. This is one reason why scientists think they may have been an ancestor of mammals.

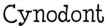

Megazostrodon

Pronounced: Meg-ah-zo-stroh-don

Megazostrodon evolved from Cynodont. Experts believe the creature was the last step between 'mammal-like' reptiles, such as cynodonts, and true mammals because, like mammals, Megazostrodon was warm-blooded.

Dicynodont

Pronounced: Die-sigh-no-dont

Dicynodonts were therapsids, or mammal-like reptiles. They looked like pigs or hippos, but they had a beak like a turtle and two tusks in their upper jaw, as have walruses - hence their name, which means 'two dog teeth'.

Allosaurus

Pronounced: Al-oh-sore-us

About 46 Allosauruses have been found in the Cleveland Lloyd Quarry in Utah, USA. Scientists think that both herbivorous and some carnivorous dinosaurs became trapped in the mud, and that the Allosauruses, seeking an easy meal, met the same fate!

Diplodocus

Pronounced: Dip-low-doe-kuss

For almost 100 years, (Dippy) the Diplodocus skeleton at the Natural History Museum in London stood with its tail on the ground. In 1993, scientists at the museum realized the tail probably counterbalanced the neck, so it was lifted into the air.

Plateosaurus

Pronounced: Plat-ee-oh-sore-us

Adult Plateosauruses came in many different sizes: some reached 'only' 4.8 metres (16ft) in length, while others were as long as 10 metres (33ft). Scientists believe this may be because some found areas with plenty of plant life, while others weren't so successful!

Phorusrhacids (or Terror Birds)

Pronounced: For-uss-ray-kids

North and South America joined together about 3 million years ago, and at least one species of terror bird, Titanis, migrated to North America. Its remains have been found in Florida. It was 2.5 metres (8ft 2in) tall, weighed approximately 150kg (330lb) and had clawed feet that were probably used to kill its prey.

Leviathan

Pronounced: Leh-vie-ah-than

Leviathan was discovered in 2008, when a tooth-studded skull, 3 metres (10ft) long, was found in Peru. Scientists called it Leviathan after the giant monster of the Bible. However, some scientists now call it by the Hebrew name Livyatan, as the name Leviathan had already been used for a species of mastodon, a group of extinct mammals related to elephants.

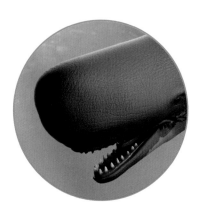

Woolly Mammoth

In May 2013, an adult female mammoth, nicknamed Buttercup, was found in a chunk of ice in Siberia. She was 40,000 years old but was still so well-preserved that even her blood was found in muscle tissue. In true Jurassic Park style, scientists think they may be able to clone a new mammoth from the DNA in the blood.

Diprotodon

Pronounced: Die-pro-toe-don

Marsupial mammals originated in South America. About 55 million years ago, they travelled to Australia via Antarctica as all three continents were linked. When marsupials are first born their eyes, ears and rear limbs hardly exist. However, their front limbs, nostrils and mouths are well developed. This allows them to crawl to their mother's pouch and drink her milk so they keep growing.

INDEX

INDEX

THE AUTHOR
Matthew Rake lives in London and has worked in publishing for more than 20 years. He has written on a wide variety of topics, including science, sports and the arts.

THE ARTIST
Peter Minister started out as a special-effects sculptor and had an exciting career producing sculptures and props for museums, theme parks, TV and film. He now works in CGI, which allows him to express himself with a big ball of digital clay in a more creative way than any 'real' clay. His CGI dinosaurs and other animals have appeared in numerous books worldwide.